World Book's Learning Ladders

Biggest, Fastest, Smallest, Slowest!

WORLD
BOOK

www.worldbook.com

World Book, Inc.
180 North LaSalle Street
Suite 900
Chicago, Illinois 60601
USA

For information about other World Book publications, visit our website at **www.worldbook.com** or call **1-800-WORLDBK (967-5325)**.

For information about sales to schools and libraries, call **1-800-975-3250 (United States); 1-800-837-5365 (Canada)**.

Library of Congress Cataloging-in-Publication Data for this volume has been applied for.

World Book's Learning Ladders
ISBN 978-0-7166-7945-5 (set, hc.)

Biggest, Fastest, Smallest, Slowest!
ISBN 978-0-7166-7946-2 (hc.)

Also available as:
ISBN 978-0-7166-7956-1 (e-book)

Printed in China by Shenzhen Wing King Tong Paper Products Co, Ltd., Shenzhen, Guangdong
1st printing December 2017

Staff

Executive Committee
President: Jim O'Rourke
Vice President and Editor in Chief: Paul A. Kobasa
Vice President, Finance: Donald D. Keller
Vice President, Marketing: Jean Lin
Vice President, International Sales: Maksim Rutenberg
Vice President, Technology: Jason Dole
Director, Human Resources: Bev Ecker

Editorial
Director, New Print Publishing: Tom Evans
Senior Editor, New Print Publishing: Shawn Brennan
Writer: Echo Elise González
Director, Digital Product Content Development: Emily Kline
Manager, Indexing Services: David Pofelski
Manager, Contracts & Compliance (Rights & Permissions):
  Loranne K. Shields
Librarian: S. Thomas Richardson

Digital
Director, Digital Product Development: Erika Meller
Digital Product Manager: Jonathan Wills

Graphics and Design
Senior Art Director: Tom Evans
Coordinator, Design Development and Production: Brenda Tropinski
Senior Visual Communications Designer: Melanie J. Bender
Media Researcher: Rosalia Bledsoe

Manufacturing/Pre-Press
Manufacturing Manager: Anne Fritzinger
Proofreader: Nathalie Strassheim

What's inside?

This book tells you about some animals that are big, small, fast, or slow! You can find out what size these animals are, what they like to eat, and how fast they can—or don't—move!

Blue whale

biggest mammal

The blue whale is the biggest animal that has ever lived. It is longer than 2 buses and weighs more than 20 elephants! It lives in the water, but it is not a fish. It is a mammal (an animal that feeds its young with milk). There are blue whales in every ocean in the world.

The **mouth** opens up wide to take in lots of water and food.

Bendable **baleen** strips hang from each side of its mouth. The strips catch food from the water.

The main food of the blue whale is a tiny shrimplike animal called **krill.**

The **tongue** weighs as much as an elephant!

The blue whale's throat skin has many **grooves** so it can stretch like a huge balloon when it is time to eat.

When a blue whale swims to the water's surface to breathe air, it spouts water up through its **blowhole.** The water can reach up to 40 feet (12 meters) high!

The blue whale moves through the water by waving its strong **tail** up and down.

It's a fact!

A blue whale can eat 40 million krill in one day!

Bumblebee bat

smallest mammal

The bumblebee bat is the smallest mammal. It is about the size of a large bumblebee—that's how the bat got its name! Bumblebee bats live deep inside caves in Southeast Asia. They come out at night to find insects and spiders to eat.

The bumblebee bat can **hear** sounds that are too high for humans to hear.

It's a fact!

Bumblebee bats use sound to figure out what is around them. They squeak and then listen for the echoes that bounce back.

Webbed hand bones are used as **wings** for flying.

The thumbs have little **claws** for hooking and grabbing.

The bumblebee bat is also called the "hognose bat" because its **nose** looks like a pig's nose.

The bumblebee bat hangs upside-down while resting.

Soft, warm **fur** keeps the small body warm.

This tiny bat weighs only about as much as two raisins!

Sloth

slowest land animal

The sloth is the slowest land animal. It does everything slowly! The sloth spends most of its life in trees. It lives in rain forests in Central and South America. Leaves, fruits, and twigs are its favorite things to eat. The sloth spends most of its time hanging upside down!

The sloth uses its long **claws** to hold onto tree branches.

The **legs** are best used for hanging from tree limbs, not walking.

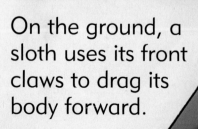

On the ground, a sloth uses its front claws to drag its body forward.

The long **arms** are good for swimming in water.

The sloth uses its hard **lips** to tear leaves to eat.

The sloth's **hair** is thick and long. Bugs and green algae (a small type of living thing) live in the sloth's hair.

It's a fact!

Most humans can walk 1 mile (1.5 kilometers) in about 20 minutes. A sloth would take more than 6 hours to go the same distance!

Cheetah

fastest land animal

The cheetah is faster than any other land animal. This big cat can run as fast as the cars move on a highway! Cheetahs live in the grasslands of Africa. They run fast so they can catch animals to eat. Cheetahs eat gazelles, wildebeests, hares, and other fast-moving animals.

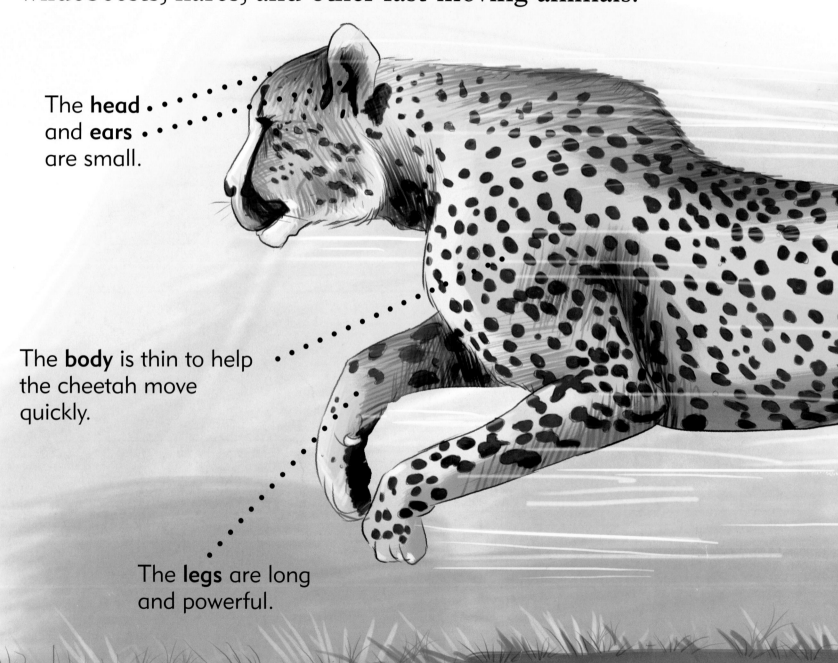

The **head** and **ears** are small.

The **body** is thin to help the cheetah move quickly.

The **legs** are long and powerful.

It's a fact!

The word *cheetah* comes from the Hindi word *chita*, which means *spotted* or *sprinkled*.

Cheetah cubs learn to hunt by playing with each other. As they grow up, they can run faster and faster.

The cheetah uses its long **tail** to stay balanced during quick turns.

The cheetah digs its **claws** into the ground to run faster.

Saltwater crocodile

biggest reptile

The saltwater crocodile is the biggest reptile in the world. A reptile is an animal with dry, scaly skin that has lungs for breathing. The saltwater crocodile lives in the salty waters around Australia and some parts of Asia. It can grow to be longer than 4 bathtubs placed end-to-end! It can be as heavy as a bull! Many people who live in Australia call these crocodiles *salties*.

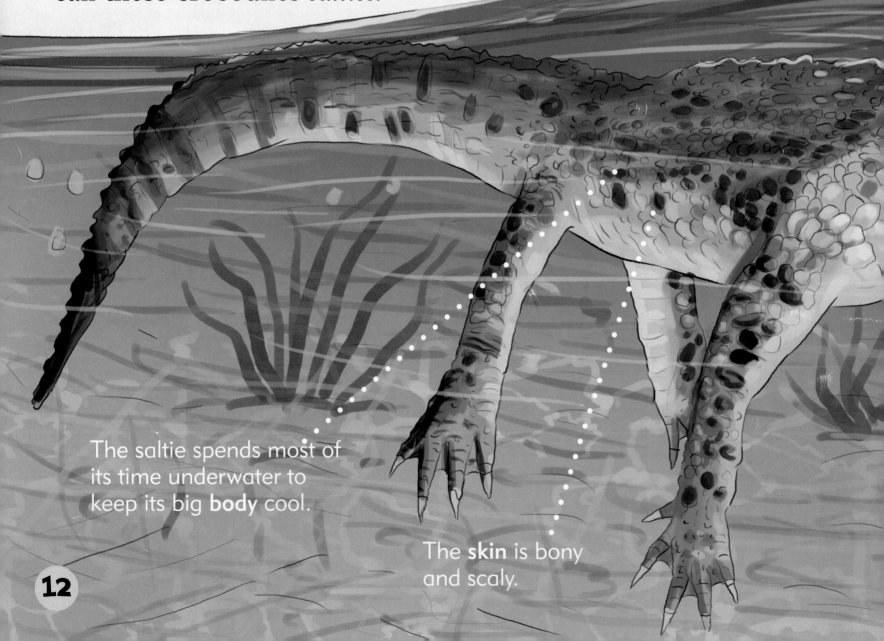

The saltie spends most of its time underwater to keep its big **body** cool.

The **skin** is bony and scaly.

It's a fact!

Saltwater crocodiles hunt and eat many different animals, including sharks and monkeys!

When hunting for food, the saltie hides underwater and then jumps out, snapping its huge jaws!

The **eyes** are on top of the head so the sneaky saltie can see above the water.

The **jaws** are very long and have many sharp **teeth.**

A mother saltwater crocodile can lay up to 90 eggs at one time.

The **feet** are webbed to help it swim.

Leaf chameleon

The leaf chameleon is a very tiny lizard. It is the smallest reptile in the world. It weighs less than one paper clip! Leaf chameleons live on the forest floor on an island that is part of the African country of Madagascar. They hide under dead leaves and hunt for tiny insects to eat.

The leaf chameleon uses its strong **tail** as an extra leg to stay balanced.

It's a fact!

Chameleons can change the color and pattern of their skin.

The **feet** grab like tiny hands.

14

The sides of the **body** are flat, which makes the chameleon hard to see.

A baby leaf chameleon can fit on the tip of a finger!

The **eyes** move around separately. This lizard can look forward and backward at the same time!

The long, sticky **tongue** catches insects to eat.

Sailfish fastest fish

The sailfish is the fastest fish. It can swim faster than a speedboat. It uses its speed to hunt for tuna, sardines, squids, and other underwater creatures. It is called a sailfish because its dorsal fin (top fin) is big, like a sailboat's sail. Sailfish live in warm ocean waters around the world.

The **dorsal fin** is used like a boat sail, to help the sailfish make sharp turns.

The **forked tail** swishes from side to side as the sailfish swims.

The **body** is long and thin to help the sailfish quickly swim through the water.

The sailfish brings its **pelvic fin** (bottom fin) close to its body when it swims fast.

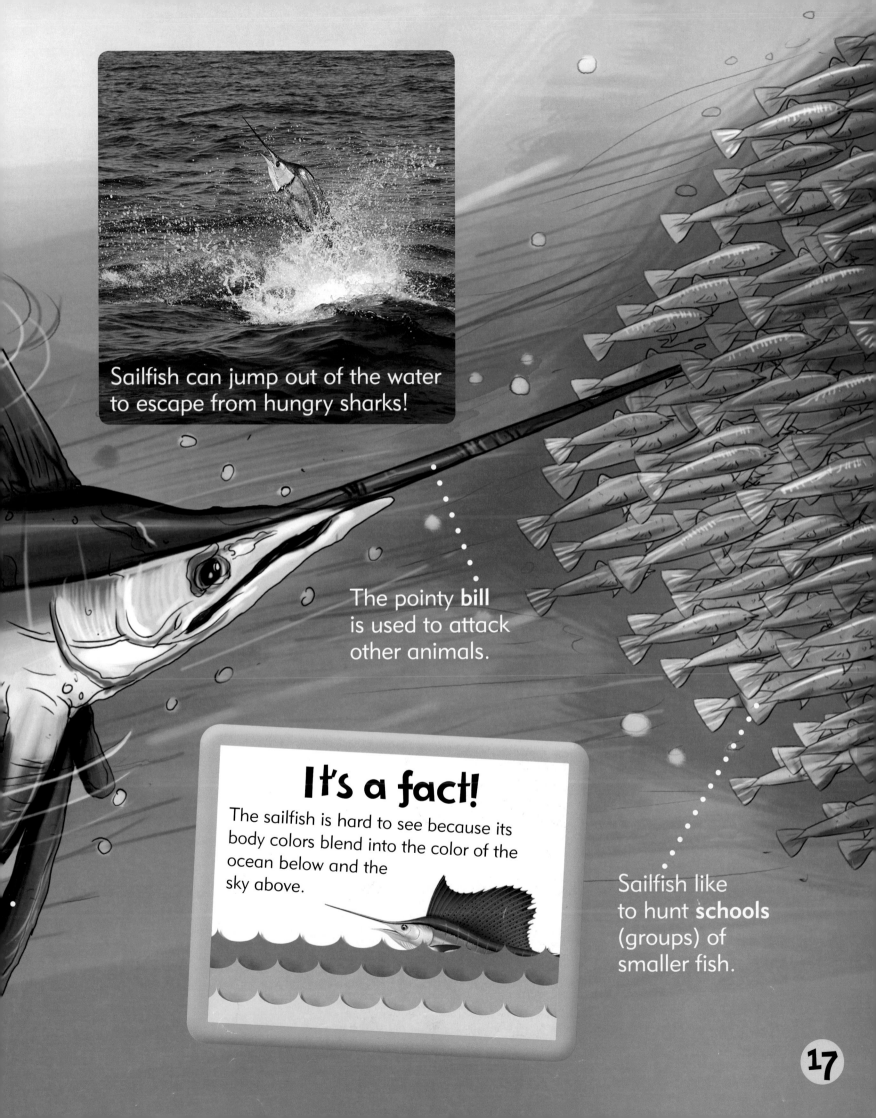

Sailfish can jump out of the water to escape from hungry sharks!

The pointy **bill** is used to attack other animals.

It's a fact!

The sailfish is hard to see because its body colors blend into the color of the ocean below and the sky above.

Sailfish like to hunt **schools** (groups) of smaller fish.

Dwarf seahorse

slowest fish

The dwarf seahorse is the slowest of all fish. It is so slow that it travels only 5 feet (1.5 meters) in one hour! The dwarf seahorse lives in sea grass at the bottom of the Atlantic Ocean. It grabs the sea grass with its tail and waits for tiny animals to pass by. Then, it sucks them up into its tube-shaped mouth.

It's a fact!

The dwarf seahorse is one of the smallest seahorses. It grows to be about 1 inch (2.5 centimeters) long.

Dwarf seahorses can change their body color to match what is around them.

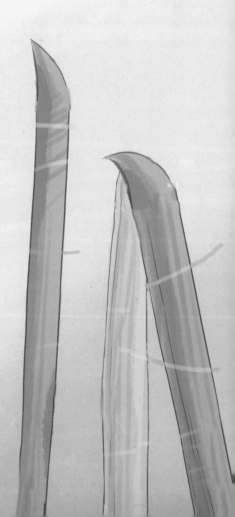

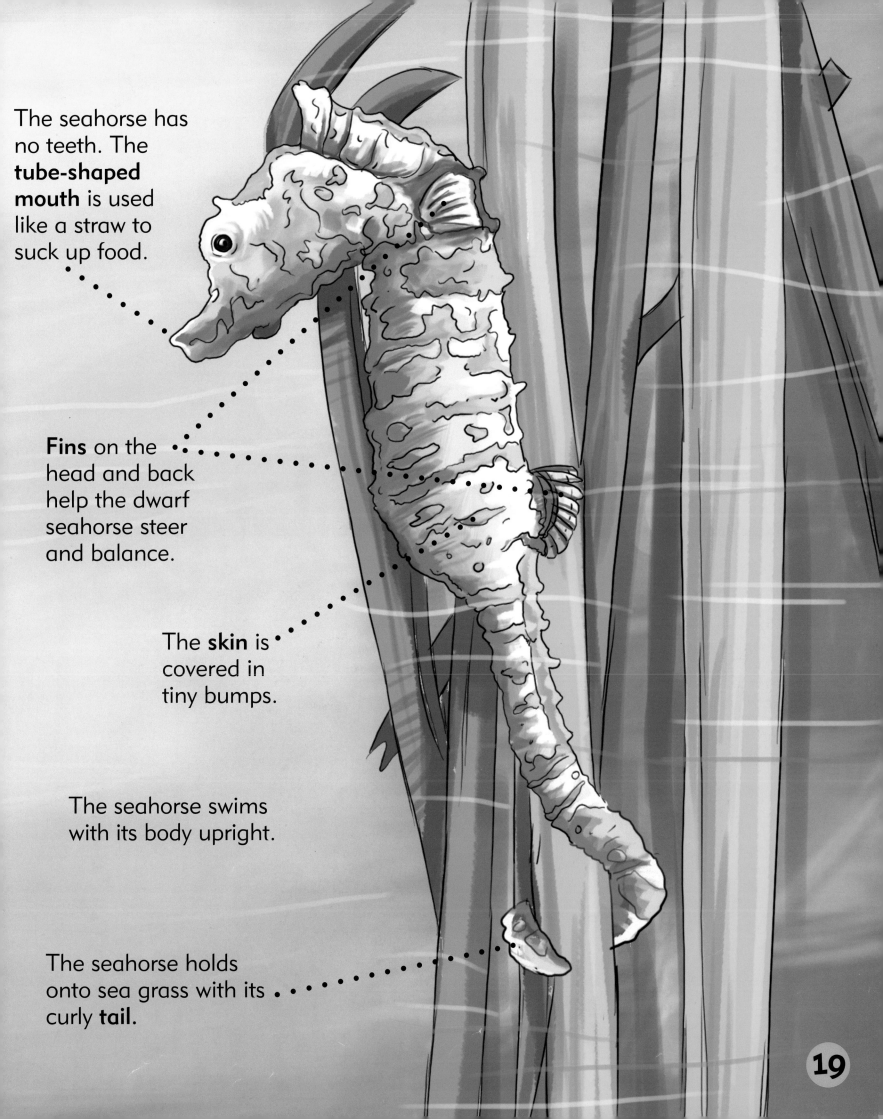

The seahorse has no teeth. The **tube-shaped mouth** is used like a straw to suck up food.

Fins on the head and back help the dwarf seahorse steer and balance.

The **skin** is covered in tiny bumps.

The seahorse swims with its body upright.

The seahorse holds onto sea grass with its curly **tail**.

Ostrich
biggest bird

The ostrich is the biggest bird in the world. It is as tall as some grown-up basketball players! It has wings, but it is too big and too heavy to fly. Ostriches roam the sandy areas of Africa, where they eat grasses, flowers, seeds, and small animals.

Ostriches have the biggest **eyes** of any land animal.

The body is covered in fluffy, soft **feathers**. . . . .

It's a fact!

Ostrich eggs are the biggest eggs in the world. Eating one ostrich egg for breakfast would be like eating two dozen chicken eggs!

The **long** neck helps the ostrich see danger from far away.

Powerful **legs** help the ostrich run fast and far. An ostrich can run up to 40 miles (64 kilometers) per hour!

Strong **claws** can be used to attack predators (hunting animals).

Ostriches share their home with giraffes and many other animals in Africa.

Ostriches like to take dust baths to get oil and bugs out of their feathers.

Bee hummingbird

The bee hummingbird is the smallest of all birds. It is shorter than your pinky finger! Bee hummingbirds live in Cuba, a Caribbean island, where they spend their time flying from flower to flower.

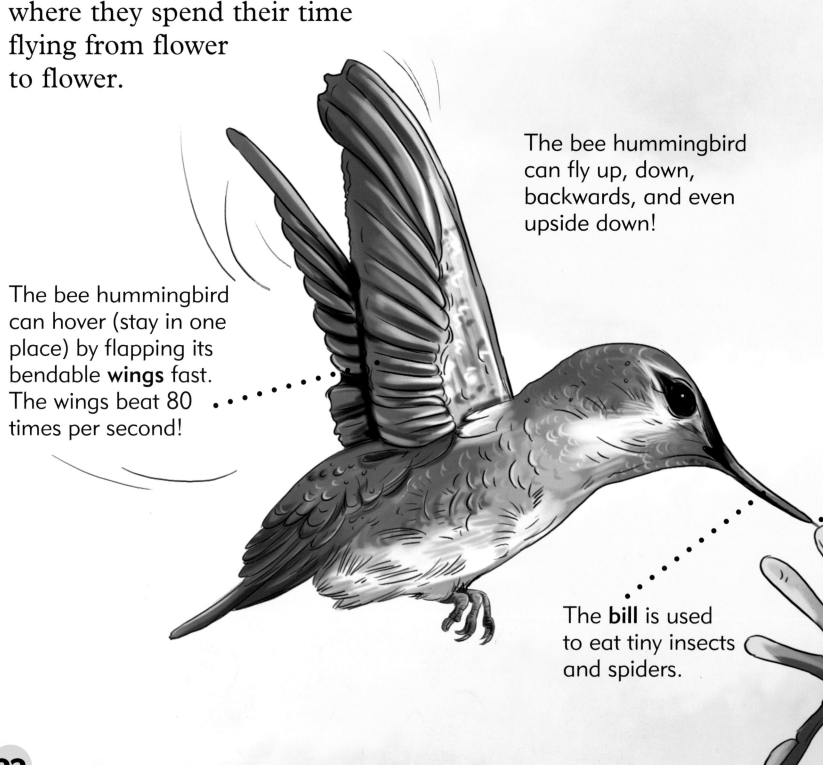

The bee hummingbird can fly up, down, backwards, and even upside down!

The bee hummingbird can hover (stay in one place) by flapping its bendable **wings** fast. The wings beat 80 times per second!

The **bill** is used to eat tiny insects and spiders.

22

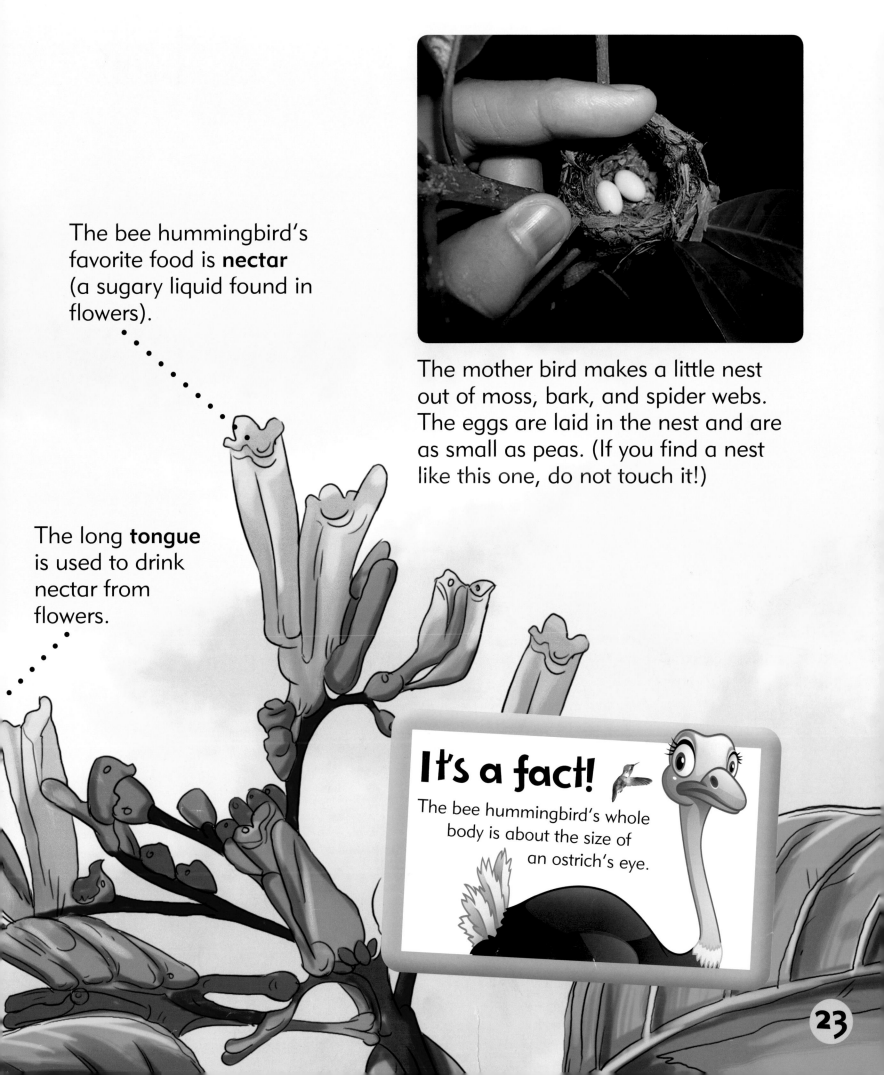

The bee hummingbird's favorite food is **nectar** (a sugary liquid found in flowers).

The long **tongue** is used to drink nectar from flowers.

The mother bird makes a little nest out of moss, bark, and spider webs. The eggs are laid in the nest and are as small as peas. (If you find a nest like this one, do not touch it!)

It's a fact!

The bee hummingbird's whole body is about the size of an ostrich's eye.

Speed and Size

There are many animals in the world. Some are big and some are small. Some are fast and some are slow.

Speed

Words you know

Here are some words that you read earlier in this book. Say them out loud, then try to find the things in the picture.

claw   wing
tail   skin
fin   bill

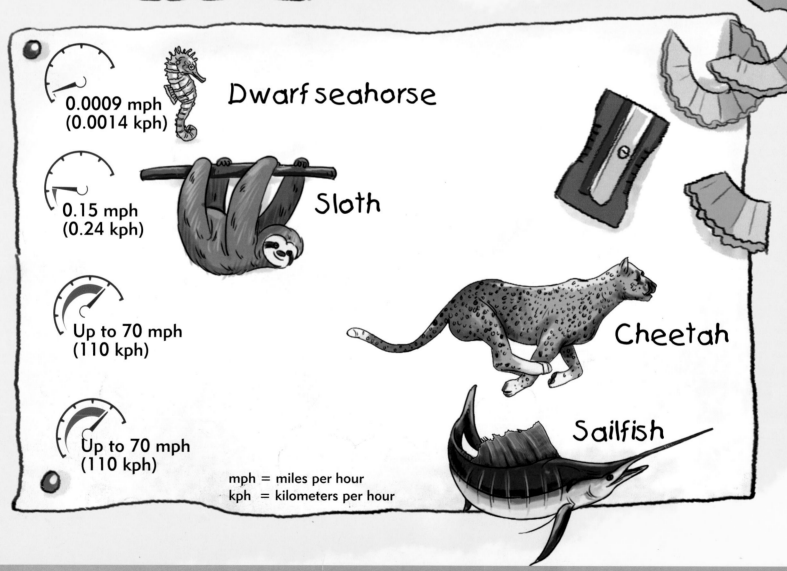

0.0009 mph
(0.0014 kph)
Dwarf seahorse

0.15 mph
(0.24 kph)
Sloth

Up to 70 mph
(110 kph)

Up to 70 mph
(110 kph)

Cheetah

Sailfish

mph = miles per hour
kph = kilometers per hour

24

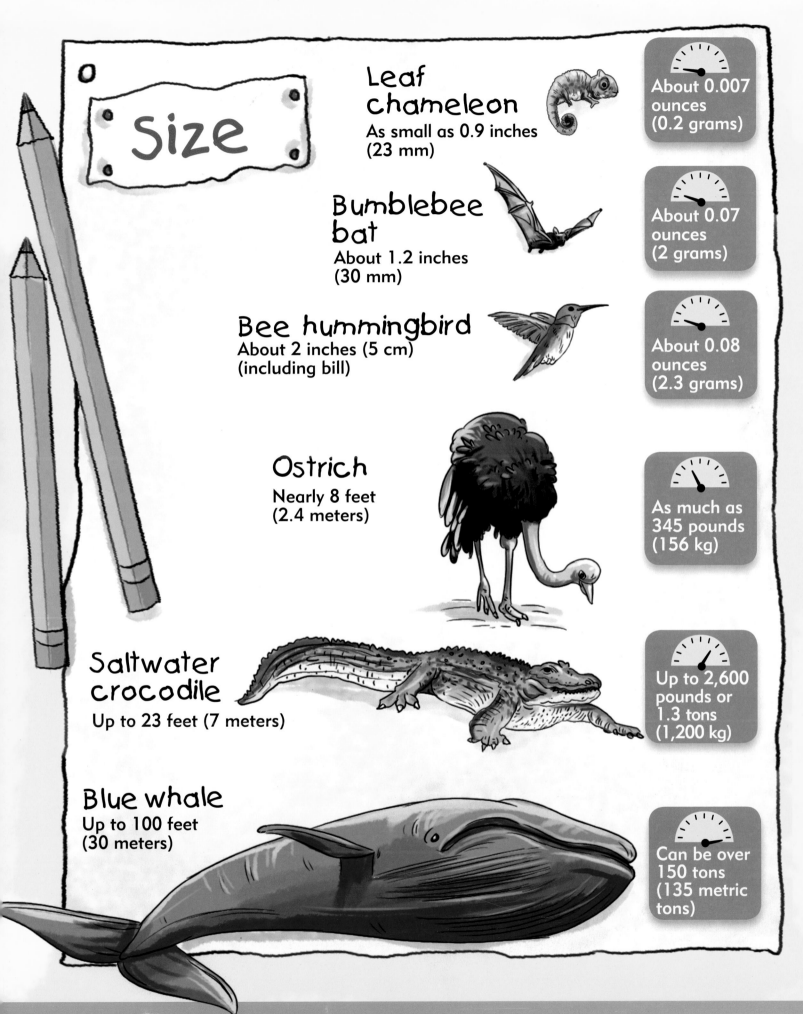

Size

Leaf chameleon
As small as 0.9 inches (23 mm)

About 0.007 ounces (0.2 grams)

Bumblebee bat
About 1.2 inches (30 mm)

About 0.07 ounces (2 grams)

Bee hummingbird
About 2 inches (5 cm) (including bill)

About 0.08 ounces (2.3 grams)

Ostrich
Nearly 8 feet (2.4 meters)

As much as 345 pounds (156 kg)

Saltwater crocodile
Up to 23 feet (7 meters)

Up to 2,600 pounds or 1.3 tons (1,200 kg)

Blue whale
Up to 100 feet (30 meters)

Can be over 150 tons (135 metric tons)

How many animals have wings?

25

Did you know?

The smallest frog is about the size of a housefly.

The proboscis (*proh BOS ihs*) monkey has the biggest nose of any monkey.

The African elephant is the biggest land animal. It also has the biggest ears and the biggest teeth of any animal.

The biggest parrot is the kakapo *(KAH kuh poh)*. It does not fly.

The tallest land animal is the giraffe. It also has the longest neck and the longest tail.

The giant clam can have thousands of eyes! It has the most eyes of any animal.

Puzzles

Close-up!

We've zoomed in on three different animals. Can you figure out which animal you are looking at?

1

2

3

Answers on page 32.

Where's home?

Can you match each animal to its home? Follow the lines to find out!

Bumblebee bat   **Dwarf seahorse**   **Sloth**

jungle   cave   sea grass

Match up!

Match each word on the left with its picture on the right.

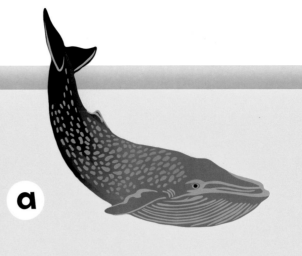

a

1. blue whale

b

2. leaf chameleon

c

3. ostrich

4. sailfish

d

5. bee hummingbird

e

6. saltwater crocodile

f

Answers on page 32.

True or false

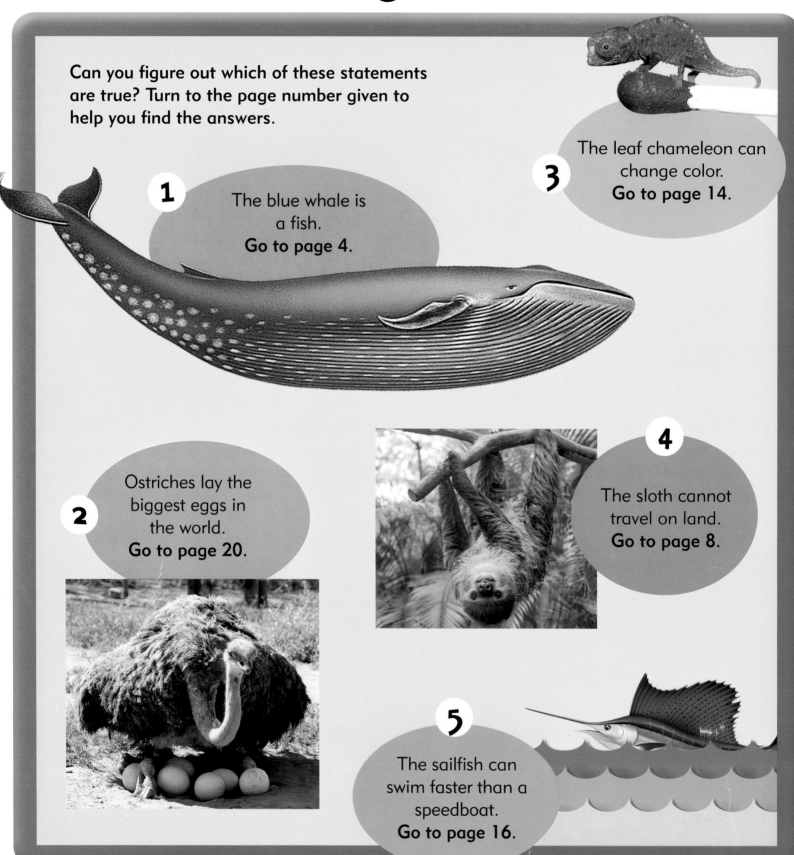

Can you figure out which of these statements are true? Turn to the page number given to help you find the answers.

1 The blue whale is a fish.
Go to page 4.

2 Ostriches lay the biggest eggs in the world.
Go to page 20.

3 The leaf chameleon can change color.
Go to page 14.

4 The sloth cannot travel on land.
Go to page 8.

5 The sailfish can swim faster than a speedboat.
Go to page 16.

Answers on page 32.

Find out more

Books

The Animal Book by Steve Jenkins (Houghton Mifflin Harcourt, 2013)
This beautifully illustrated book is loaded with fascinating facts and infographics on more than 300 animals. Includes an animal index, a glossary, and a bibliography.

Animal Encyclopedia by the U.S. National Geographic Society Staff (National Geographic Society, 2012)
This book covers 2,500 animal species and is packed with more than 3,000 stunning color photographs, amazing animal facts, maps, and more. Includes feature spreads that highlight superlatives such as fastest, tallest, smallest, etc.

Animal Opposites by Cecillia Minden (Cherry Lake, 2016). Eight volumes.
Students will develop word recognition and reading skills while learning about animal opposites and habits. Series titles: *Big and Small*, *Fast and Slow*, *Hard and Soft*, *Hot and Cold*, *In and Out*, *Push and Pull*, *Sit and Stand*, and *Up and Down*.

Wild Animal Atlas by the U.S. National Geographic Society Staff (National Geographic Society, 2010)
This child-friendly atlas features stunning animal photos and colorful, easily accessible maps to teach young readers about geography through the wild creatures that fascinate them.

Websites

All About Mammals
http://www.kidzone.ws/animals/mammals.htm
Learn what makes a mammal a mammal and not some other kind of animal.

Animal Database
http://www.kidsbiology.com/animals-for-children.php
Learn about hundreds of different animals, from anteaters, armadillos, and aardvarks to songbirds, turtles, and whales on this website from Kids Biology. Each animal page includes a photograph and a list of animal facts.

Animals of the World
http://www.kidscom.com/games/animal/animal.html
KidsCom outlines the features that classify animals as insects, fish, amphibians, reptiles, birds, and mammals, and offers games to test your knowledge.

National Geographic Kids
http://kids.nationalgeographic.com/animals/
Learn about wild animals on this website from *National Geographic Kids Magazine*. Each feature includes fun facts, pictures, sound bites, videos, and a map that shows where the creature lives.

Answers

Puzzles
from pages 28 and 29

Close-up!
1. ostrich
2. crocodile
3. cheetah

Match up!
1. a
2. c
3. e
4. b
5. d
6. f

True or false
from page 30

1. false
2. true
3. true
4. false
5. true

Index